HMS HEAR MY STORY

100 YEARS,
1,000 STORIES,
1 ROYAL NAVY

Hear My Story, in the Museum's new Babcock Galleries, tells the undiscovered stories from the ordinary men, women and ships that have made the Royal Navy's amazing history over the last 100 years; the Navy's century of greatest change.

This is an exhibition where you can see and hear the stories of the Navy in war and in peace, from the storms of the Arctic to the heat of Afghanistan. Get immersed in technology to disguise your ship, hunt a submarine and send messages in code. Meet the veterans who can tell you first hand their stories of living and fighting at sea. This is an exhibition where your story matters. Take part, share precious personal memories about yourself or your family, add these stories to history and join the debate on what the future may hold.

From the start of the 20th century the Navy was at the very heart of British life. It affected millions of men and women at home and around the world. Over the last 100 years the Royal Navy has changed in its size, its role in the world, its friends and enemies. Technology has revolutionised ships and the lives of those on board. However, ships still sail, families are still left behind and crews still face the challenges of the sea. HMS Hear My Story tells this dramatic and moving story.

NAVY LIFE

CHANGING PEOPLE

Just like society, the Navy is constantly changing. Each new generation needs different specialist and technical skills. People change in the Navy too, but what they learn, what they do and what they see stays with them forever.

Imagine a crew from 1914 joining a ship today. What would the old Gun Layer say to the new Warfare Specialist? Could the Pusser help the Logistics Officer supply the ship? How would the Captain lead the women in his crew?

▼ The crew of HMS *Swiftsure* in 1914.

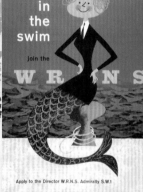

NAVY LIVES

A Bank Clerk Goes to Sea

Phillip Needell was working in a London bank when the Navy called him up in the First World War. He left behind his young wife and two-year-old daughter to spend three years patrolling the seas. Like hundreds of thousands of other reservists, Needell had to adapt to a new life. With his quick brain and good eyesight he was the perfect Signalman and joined HMS *Alamanzora*. At first, his ship blockaded the North Atlantic to stop essential war supplies getting to Germany. Later, it escorted merchant ships to Canada, Brazil and Sierra Leone. Needell faced icebergs, German U-boats – one of which killed a close friend – and an influenza epidemic on board. However, he loved being part of the crew and designed the ship's Christmas cards, magazines and even the scenery for amateur dramatics. In 1919, his challenges over, Phillip Needell returned to the bank and normal life.

'A hunting we will go'

Captain Frederic 'Johnnie' Walker was the Navy's greatest submarine killer. The groups he commanded sank 21 German U-boats. Walker was an innovator in tactics and a master of new technology. Instead of simply escorting convoys to safety, he actively hunted submarines. Rushing his ships to any suspected U-boat contact, he chased and attacked with depth charges, gunfire or ramming. No one had more experience as an anti-submarine specialist, but having been 'passed over' for promotion before the Second World War, Walker had to wait until October 1941 for a wartime command. Success then came almost instantly, inspiring his team and all those fighting the Battle of the Atlantic. He was promoted to Captain, and marked as a future Admiral. In June 1944 Walker led 40 ships that stopped U-boats entering the English Channel and attacking D-Day shipping. For two weeks he lived on the bridge under great pressure. Days after returning, Frederic 'Johnnie' Walker died from over-work, strain and war weariness.

A Mobile Mechanic

When Marie Callanan joined the Women's Royal Naval Service (WRNS) in 1943 she took on a crucial technical job, 'to free a man for the fleet'. Like 1,400 other women she became a Radio Mechanic, maintaining and checking the vital communication radios for ships and naval aircraft. Callanan's School Certificate in mathematics and physics was an essential qualification, but she also faced the longest training of any WRNS job before she could start. The usual two years' training was crammed into just seven months of war. Once qualified, Callanan worked in a small team, alongside men, on the radios at the Gunnery School in Plymouth. Radio Mechanics in the Second World War also worked on the radios in destroyers, and in Walrus, Barracuda and Swordfish aircraft. Some became airborne and tested the radios in flight. Marie was a 'mobile' Wren, so she moved around the country. For three years she lived with other Wrens – in a hotel, huts and a converted orphanage – receiving 3 shillings 7 pence a day.

From Snotty to Sea Lord

Frank Twiss grew up from a frightened, exhilarated, proud and humbled Snotty* who first walked aboard a battleship aged 17, to become Second Sea Lord, responsible for 100,000 men and women. Throughout his 47 years of service Twiss never knew where the next step would take him, or what challenges it would bring. He specialised as a gunnery officer, survived three years as prisoner of war to the Japanese, became an expert in nuclear radiation and, finally, ended his career at sea as Commander-in-Chief, Far East Fleet, fighting Communist forces in Borneo. With each new job, Twiss gained experience and skills. As Second Sea Lord he used all this experience to adapt the Navy. He believed that rum had no place in a modern, technological navy, for instance, and so abolished the daily ration. Looking back though, he did admit that, '... the Navy may be leaner and fitter, but it certainly is not so much fun'.

*Snotty: a Midshipman

CHANGING PLACES

Crews have always lived, worked and fought together, crammed in small boxes floating on the sea. Over time ships might change shape and look different, but the realities of life on board don't change much. Sailors still need a sense of humour, they still rely on each other and have to handle whatever is thrown at them. Can you imagine changing places with them?

▶ On the mess deck of HMS *Iroquois*, c.1945.

▼ Bunks on HMS *Intrepid*, 1968. Occupied.

Beira Bucket

Between 1966 and 1975 the Navy patrolled off the port of Beira in Mozambique to enforce a United Nations oil embargo of Rhodesia (modern-day Zimbabwe). Patrols lasted four to six weeks and the boredom of often uneventful deployments was broken by sports events during handover days. The old 'Dhoby' bucket seen here was offered by HMS *Diamond* as a trophy. Over the years, the various holders 'decorated' the bucket and it now bears the names and trophies of many of the ships that served in the waters off Beira.

'... marrowfat peas, haricot beans, corned beef, tinned meat, tinned sausages, potmess ... You either paid big whacks out of your pocket to finish your mess bill off or, if there was money to pay change, you got a mess credit ...'
Leonard McDonald, Royal Marine serving on HMS *Howe*, 1945

CHANGING FAMILIES

AU REVOIR.   G.M.PAYNE.

You didn't have to join the Navy for it to change your life. Imagine how you would feel if someone you loved was in a war zone, or away from home for months, even years? Naval families have often had to cope without husbands, fathers, wives or mothers who were away at sea. Today, the Navy gives more support to help people cope with the challenges of service life. There are benefits to being in a service family too – housing, travel abroad or just the sense of being part of the bigger naval family.

My Dearest Love

In November 1895 Chief Stoker Walter Grainger said goodbye to his fiancée Edith and sailed to join his ship on the China Station. During the three years he was away he missed Edith desperately and poured out his heart to her in hundreds of letters home. He wrote of his pain at being apart from her, how important Edith's letters were to him, and his unhappiness at being in the Navy. Yet he also illustrated each with beautiful drawings of flowers, of places he visited and of his ship, HMS *Daphne*. The letters clearly kept Edith and Walter's love alive. The couple got married on his return and had a family. Over 90 years later, their daughter gave these letters to the Museum.

Until recently, Navy letters could take weeks to arrive home. Mobile phones and email thankfully now make it easier to stay in touch, and only operational requirements restrict daily communication.

◀ The banner made by families of HMS *Dragon* to welcome the ship home from deployment in the Persian Gulf, 2013.

'We did try and use FaceTime™ but that didn't work out because as soon as she saw us she cried, the kids cried, so we're not going to do that again …'

Henry Gunner, husband of HMS *Dragon* crew member

1916

'We had been steaming at a furious speed all night. Gradually, black smudges became visible on the horizon. We could just make out the enemy line – by the sun glinting on their sides – and by the flashes of their guns.'

1943

'We got that contact at 5.30 one night. We didn't sink that U-boat until the next morning. He kept turning. We dogged him. We didn't attack, we waited. He probably thought he was away … finally about 6.30 we closed in, attacked him and got him.'

'That was when I learned the term "goalkeeper" – I asked somebody what it meant and he said: "We've got to catch anything and everything that they throw at us." … if they had started hitting amphibious ships, or the shore where the troops were trying to land, it would've been a very different day.'

1982

THE BATTLE OF JUTLAND

▲ HMS *Birmingham* under fire.

On 31 May 1916, Britain's Grand Fleet clashed with the German High Seas Fleet in the North Sea. 'Jutland' became the largest sea battle of the First World War. The German plan to ambush part of the Grand Fleet failed because the British de-coded their radio messages in advance. Battle commenced between the battlecruisers with heavy British losses, but when the main fleets joined together the weaker German force had to flee. It was not the crushing victory that the Royal Navy and British public – raised on the traditions of Nelson and Trafalgar – had hoped for. The Navy lost more men and more ships, but it was the German High Seas Fleet who decided not to risk battle again. Instead, the war became one of starvation. The Germans turned again to the U-boat, sinking British merchant ships to try and starve Britain. The Navy, in turn, slowly strangled Germany with its own economic blockade.

THE LONGEST BATTLE

▲ The Flower-class corvette HMS *Charlock*.

The Battle of the Atlantic was the longest campaign of the Second World War. For over five gruelling years, convoys of ships crossed the Atlantic, fighting Germany's U-boats in a grim, exhausting struggle. For Britain this was a battle for national survival. The German submarines were trying to sink Allied merchant ships carrying the food, weapons and supplies that were needed to keep Britain fighting. The Navy's job was to protect the convoys, attacking and harassing U-boats at every turn. The years from 1940 to 1943 were especially desperate – U-boats sank 956 British merchant ships in 1942 alone. However, in the spring and summer of 1943 a series of major convoy battles turned the tide. Although the U-boats fought on, the Germans had lost the battle after May 1943. This success allowed the Allies to build up forces and supplies for D-Day and the final liberation of Europe.

THE FALKLANDS WAR

On 2 April 1982 Argentina invaded the Falkland Islands. To recapture them, the Navy had to overcome Argentinian forces, the stormy seas of the South Atlantic and the challenges of fighting 8,000 miles away from home. A Task Force of over 100 ships had to carry everything south to the Islands. When HMS *Conqueror* sank the *General Belgrano* the threat from Argentina's navy diminished. However, for all the fighting success of the Sea Harriers, the Task Force faced constant danger from enemy aircraft. Once there, the ships had to land troops in hostile territory. The landings started successfully on 21 May and the Royal Marines famously 'yomped' to the capital. By 14 June the islands were free, but the Navy paid a heavy price. Argentina's aircraft sank the ships *Sheffield*, *Ardent*, *Antelope* and *Coventry*, many others were severely damaged, and there were 255 British casualties. The Royal Navy still defends the Islands; Argentina still maintains its claim.

▲ HMS *Coventry*, 25 May 1982.

UNFINISHED BUSINESS

The two short, intense Gulf Wars stand 13 years apart: in 1991 and 2003. The wars are linked, and both were fought by international coalitions, but the Royal Navy's part in each differed. Iraqi troops invaded Kuwait in 1990. When Iraq's President Saddam Hussein refused the United Nations' demands to leave, the United States led 34 countries into military operations. Although Saddam was forced out he remained in power. In 2003, after international controversy over the existence of Iraq's weapons of mass destruction, a US-led coalition again went to war – this time without a UN resolution. In 1991 the Navy cleared mines, gave logistical support and defended the ships from air attack. Helicopters sank Iraqi vessels, and submarines are rumoured to have landed Special Forces. The Navy's forces in 2003 were much larger: helicopters from *Ark Royal* and *Ocean* landed Royal Marines, helped with reconnaissance, or attacked land forces. This time, submarines fired Tomahawk missiles at inland targets. Major combat operations ended in April 2003, but UK forces stayed ashore until 2010.

▲ Royal Marines of Delta Company on board HMS *Ark Royal*.

THE ORIGINAL WORLD SERVICE

The Navy has been everywhere. After all, around 71% of the world is covered by oceans and over 70% of the world's population live within 150 kilometres of the coast. The Royal Navy has even reached hundreds of kilometres inland using boats, aircraft or trains to do whatever job Britain has demanded. By influencing trade and whole economies, the Navy's ships have exerted power even when they are out of sight.

River Gunboat

This model of the river gunboat HMS *Falcon* was made by a Chinese member of the crew when the ship was protecting British trade hundreds of miles up the Yangtze River in 1938. He gave it to Warrant Officer Arthur Whiting who brought it back to Britain.

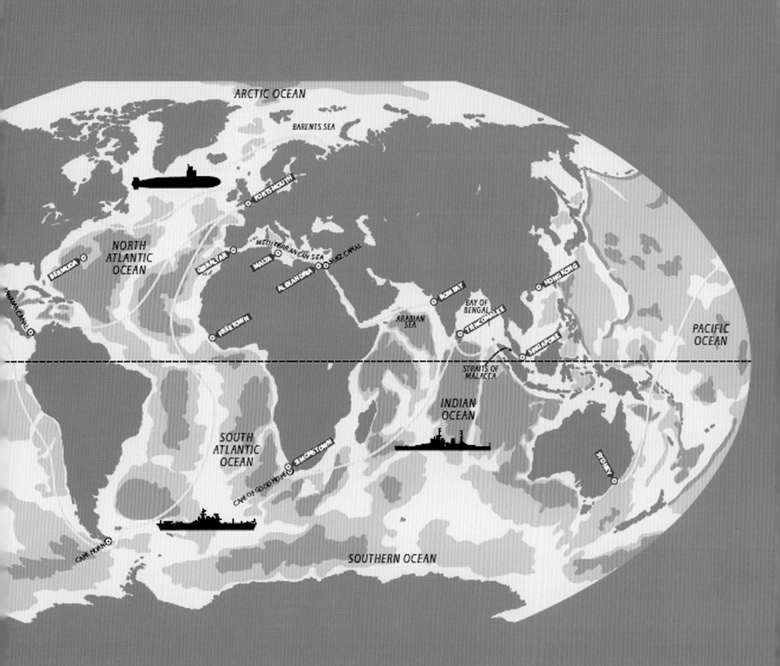

ARCTIC OCEAN

BARENTS SEA

PORTSMOUTH

NORTH
ATLANTIC
OCEAN

MEDITERRANEAN SEA

GIBRALTAR

MALTA

SUEZ CANAL

ALEXANDRIA

BERMUDA

BOMBAY

HONG KONG

PANAMA CANAL

ARABIAN
SEA

BAY OF
BENGAL

TRINCOMALEE

FREETOWN

SINGAPORE

PACIFIC
OCEAN

STRAITS OF
MALACCA

INDIAN
OCEAN

SOUTH
ATLANTIC
OCEAN

SIMONSTOWN

CAPE OF GOOD HOPE

SYDNEY

CAPE HORN

SOUTHERN OCEAN

WAR AND NOT MUCH PEACE

The Royal Navy or Royal Marines have taken part in almost every British conflict since 1900. They have helped to win world wars and – alone or with allies – have fought in many smaller conflicts. Through one long Cold War, many short hot wars and international crises, the years of peace have been few and far between. They have fought on, over and under the sea. Just as often, they have fought on and over the land too.

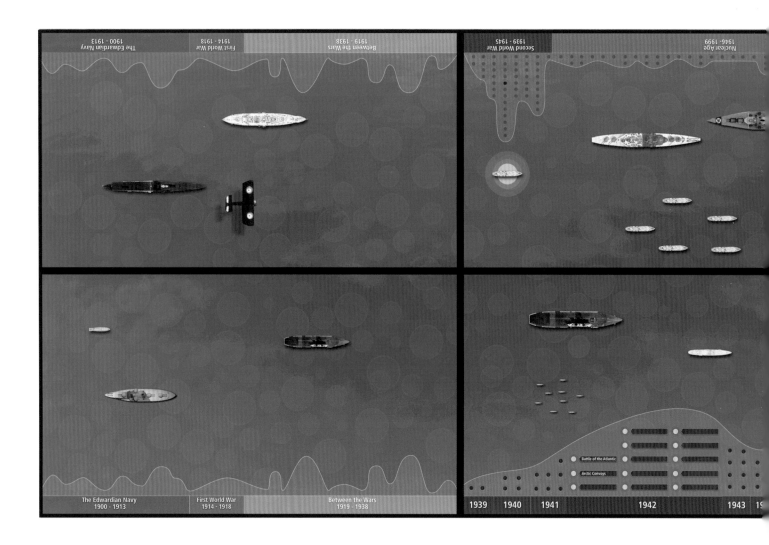

The Edwardian Navy 1900 - 1913

First World War 1914 - 1918

Between the Wars 1919 - 1938

Second World War 1939 - 1945

Nuclear Age 1946 - 1999

The Edwardian Navy 1900 - 1913

First World War 1914 - 1918

Between the Wars 1919 - 1938

Battle of the Atlantic

Arctic Convoys

| 1939 | 1940 | 1941 | 1942 | 1943 | 1 |

The story of the Navy is not only about its ships and its sailors, it's also about the Navy's changing influence on Britain. Part of this influence came from the image of the Navy in films, fashion and advertising. Into the 1970s this popular culture brought the Navy into daily life, reaching people far from the sea. The image affected how people in Britain – and overseas – thought and felt about the Navy.

Sailor Suit

Paul and Simon Dickinson, aged 3 and 4½, proudly wearing the sailor suits bought for them in 1939. The sailor suit for boys and for girls became fashionable after Prince Albert, later King Edward VII, dressed in a miniature version of the Royal Yacht uniform in 1846. Children rarely wear them now, but they still inspire fashion.

MEETING THE NAVY

t's all about showing off, and showing people a good time: royal coronations, jubilees and state visits celebrated by fleet reviews. Navy Days, with the big ships thrown open to the public, give a glimpse of life inside. Warship visits up and down the country – and all over the world – welcome everyone up the gangway. Festivities also occur at every ship launch and commissioning.

These are parties, but done with a purpose. The Navy has always had to show the British taxpayer what their money is paying for. When you are overseas, it is always useful to make friends, and demonstrate what you can do.

▼ HMS *Hood* and the searchlight display, 1935.

THE NAVY BRAND

'The Navy sets a standard for efficiency.
Peek Freen's sets the standard for biscuit making.'
Advert, 1938

Many people have tried to borrow the glamour, prestige and popularity of the Royal Navy to sell products. Over the years, makers of everything from tea to shaving foam and beer have used the power of the Navy's brand.

Consumers saw the Navy as a smart, capable and efficient service with a long tradition. Phrases like 'unequalled', 'superior quality' and 'second to none' often appeared in adverts. Suppliers of equipment to the Navy, such as fridges, used this seal of approval when selling their products direct to the public. Advertisers linked many other items including cars, razors, baby rusks and peas to the Navy, even if there was no real connection.

At the same time, film and radio have promoted the idea of the Navy's sailors as resourceful, cheerful and brave. They were also a little cheeky, and adverts for holidays or excursions to naval towns promoted this as part of their unique atmosphere.

▶ This advert for Morris motor cars dates from 1938.

▶ Showcards advertising the film
In Which We Serve directed by
Noel Coward, 1942.

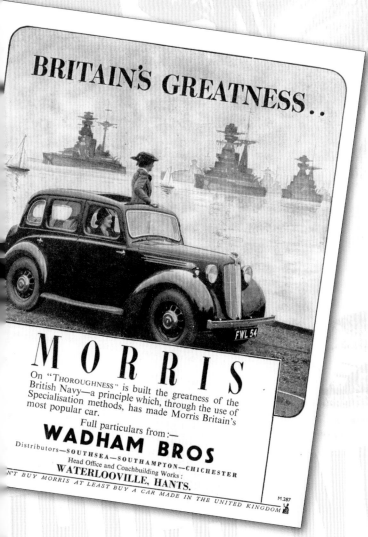

BUILDING

Every ship design is a compromise. Creating the shape – or 'platform' – best suited to a ship's job and also to carrying its weapons means balancing one capability with another. A lighter hull and more speed means less protection; big guns mean more weight, more crew and a higher cost. In the last 100 years designers have harnessed the special properties of new materials for building and new fuels for moving ships.

▼ The *Hood* was the Navy's longest ever ship. This length created a hull shape that was fast, but attempts to reduce weight gave too little armour protection.

TALKING

WIRELESS TELEGRAPHY

▲ A Wireless Telegraphist using the Morse code tapper, early 1900s. A skilled user could send 30 words a minute.

I n July 1899 three Royal Navy ships tested a new 'wireless' communication system. The test sent electromagnetic waves carrying Morse code messages 45 miles across the sea. This was revolutionary for the Navy – for the first time ships could 'talk' over long distances, without relying on visible flags or lamps – and wireless technology quickly became a permanent feature on Navy vessels. In the years since, further new technologies have changed the speed, ease and content of communication. Today, ships share complex information instantly using satellite data links.

'... there was hardly any room to work, it was very hot ... packed from the deck to the deck-head. If the ship was rolling it could be quite entertaining.'
David Lester, Radio Electrical Mechanic

Sparks Across the Sea

The Wireless Telegraphy (W/T) Office, later called the Radio Room, was where it all happened. The Telegraphist or 'Sparker' worked here deciphering incoming signals and tapping out new Morse messages. The office was designed for use by one man, so everything was in easy reach. However, this meant that dangerous voltages were also always close by and electric shocks were regarded as part of the job. This unique W/T Office from HMS *Resource* is typical of the late 1920s to early 1930s. The main transmitter sent messages up to 350 miles away.

ATTACK AND DEFENCE

Ships use weapons for attacking, and as part of their defence. In the last 100 years these have evolved many times over as scientists and engineers have created new designs and the range of fighting at sea has increased. In the past, heavy guns could only hit targets that were visible; now, missiles can travel hundreds of miles over the horizon and naval aircraft range far from ships. Weapons are also much more complex and are now integrated with all the ships' systems.

▼ The cruiser HMS *Euryalus* in the Mediterranean, 22 March 1942.

▶ HMS *Malaya* firing 15-inch guns, 1932.

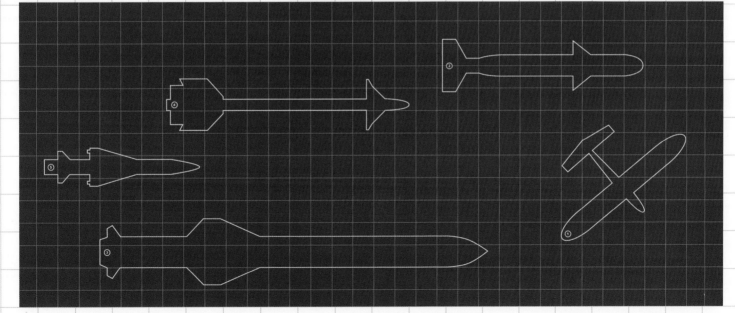

HIDING AND SEEKING

Ships and submarines are tiny when placed against the depths and distances of the sea. Hiding should be easy, but new technologies keep changing the game of hide and seek. When everything depended on a look-out's eyes, smoke, camouflage or confusing 'dazzle' paint could hide you. But aircraft, sonar and radar, which all seek out ships, made these early techniques less effective. Now there are new ways of hiding, including 'stealthy' ships whose designs avoid detection by radar. Increasingly, ships use remotely operated technology, such as the Seafox mine-disposal system, for seeking.

Submarine attacks in the First World War made it a matter of life and death for ships to be able to 'look' below the surface of the ocean. Of course for submarines it became just as vital to be able to hide. In 1917 the Navy started listening for the noise of submarines using 'hydro-phones' – simple microphones towed in the water. Today, ships, submarines and helicopters all use sophisticated versions of this technology. Experiments also started at this time with ships actively sending out pulses of sound and listening for echoes back from objects underwater – just like whales and dolphins do in nature. This became known as ASDIC and the Navy first fitted it to a ship in 1919. We know it today by its American name Sound Navigation and Ranging, or 'sonar'.

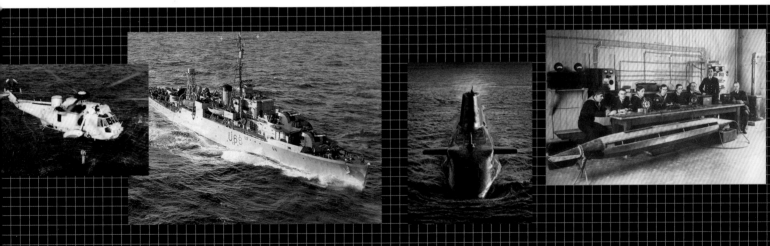

'I heard the spine-chilling cheeping notes of an ASDIC transmission in contact … followed by shattering explosions going off above us.'
Signalman Gus Britton, HM Submarine *Trident*, 1942

INTO THE FUTURE

I t's easy to predict the future – or at least the shape – of the Royal Navy's future fleet. The Navy is currently building and designing ships that will be at work up to 2050. It is harder, however, to know what demands the coming years will bring. Building versatile and agile ships, and training men and women who can cope with change, will be more important than ever.

'The challenges of the here and now mustn't obscure our ambitions for the future ...'
Admiral Sir George Zambellas, First Sea Lord, April 2013

▼ The Type 26 Frigate will come into service in 2021, to become the backbone of the fleet in the 2030s.

▲ The Royal Navy training on the Joint Strike Fighter, Florida 2013. The fighter is due to start test flights from HMS *Queen Elizabeth* in 2018.

▲ Royal Marines from RFA *Fort Victoria* capture seven suspected pirates 350 miles from Somalia's coast, 2011.

▼ The Astute-class submarine HMS *Ambush* returning to base, 2013.

HOME OF THE NAVY

HM Naval Base Portsmouth is home to 60% of the Royal Navy's surface ships. Mighty carriers, powerful destroyers and nimble patrol ships are all based here. Ships from NATO countries or allies from further afield are frequent visitors. Ships move constantly around the base for maintenance, repair and refit, or simply to take on fuel and ammunition. All are carefully controlled by the Queen's Harbour Master. See what ships you can spot as you leave the Museum today.

Paintings made by Lachlan Goudie on visits to dockyards in Rosyth and Govan to see construction of HMS *Duncan* and the new aircraft carrier HMS *Queen Elizabeth*, 2012 and 2013. ▲ 'Industry'. ◀ 'HMS *Duncan*'. ▶ 'Ready for Rosyth'.

▼ 'Bridge (Sunset)' by Jules George. Painted on board HMS *Argyll* in the Persian Gulf, November 2011.

Text written by The National Museum of the Royal Navy.
The author has asserted their moral rights.

With kind acknowledgement of the generous financial support given by all our sponsors. Thanks also to the hundreds of individuals and organisations who have assisted as advisers, donors, lenders, interviewees, veterans or volunteers.

Edited by Lindsey Smith.
Designed by Jemma Cox.

All images © National Museum of the Royal Navy, except p.30–31 and inside back cover, reproduced with permission of the artists. Graphic visualisations by Redman Design, multi-media imagery by Elbow Productions.

Every effort has been made to contact copyright holders; the publisher will be pleased to rectify any omissions in future editions.

Printed in Great Britain.
ISBN 978-1-84165-548-2   1/14

Pitkin Publishing, The History Press, The Mill, Brimscombe Port, Stroud, Gloucestershire, GL5 2QG.

Enquiries and sales: 01453 883300
Email: sales@thehistorypress.co.uk
www.thehistorypress.co.uk